Usborne

Dinosaurs Magic Painting Book

Illustrated by Federica Iossa

Designed by Brenda Cole

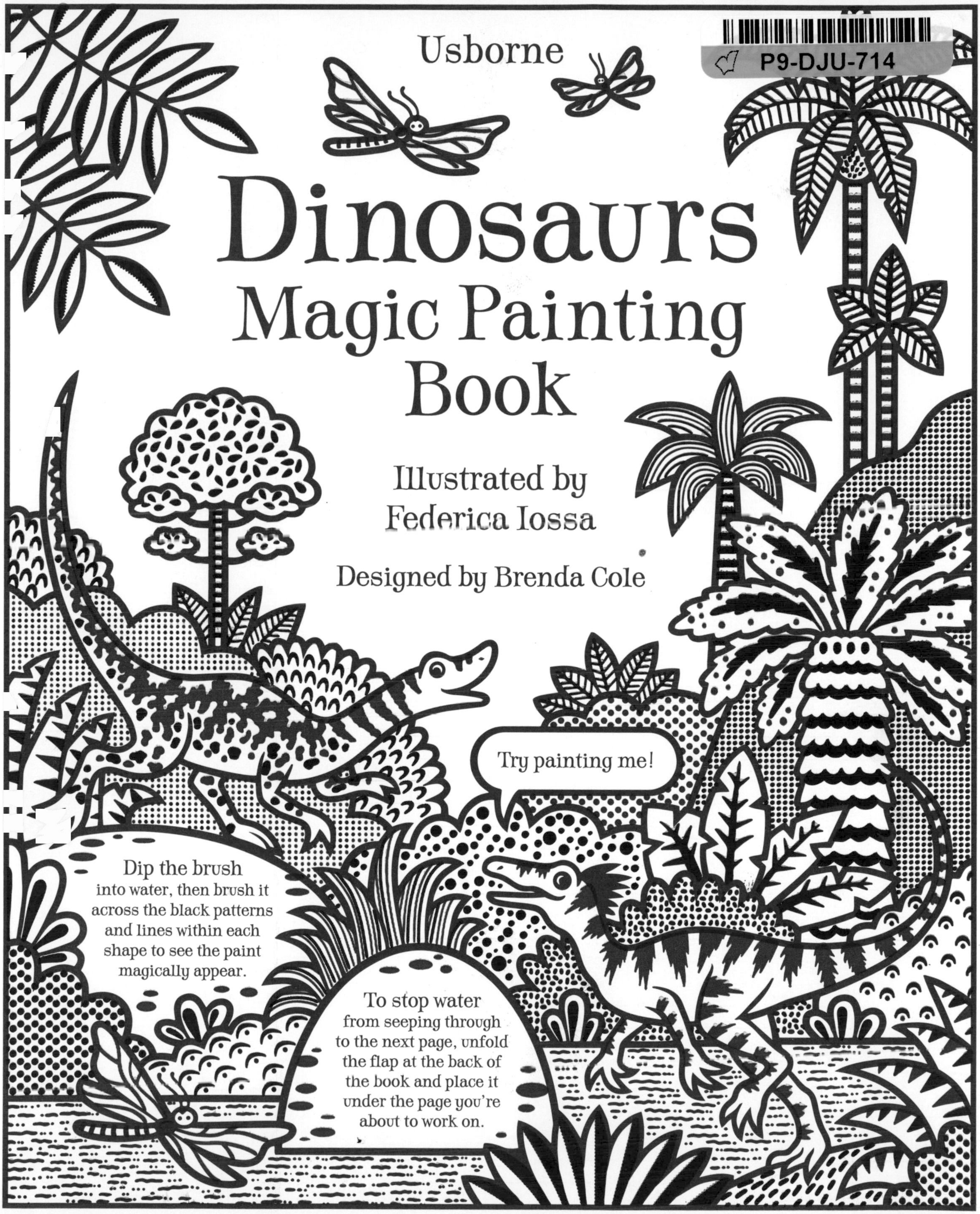

Dip the brush into water, then brush it across the black patterns and lines within each shape to see the paint magically appear.

To stop water from seeping through to the next page, unfold the flap at the back of the book and place it under the page you're about to work on.